The Pearl Diver of Irunmani

The Pearl Diver of Irunmani

Marc Vincenz

WHITE PINE PRESS / BUFFALO, NEW YORK

White Pine Press
P.O. Box 236
Buffalo, NY 14201
www.whitepine.org

Publication of this book was supported by public funds from the New
York State Council on the Arts, with the support of Governor Kathy
Hochul and the New York State Legislature, a State Agency.

Acknowledgements appear on page 138.

Cover Image: *The Aquatic Underworld*, Vietnam, 2016, by Paul Marlier

Printed and bound in the United States of America.

ISBN 978-1-945680-60-1

Library of Congress Control Number: 2022940743

The Pearl Diver of Irunmani

An Unchartable Truth

Clams

Limbo Returns

Suffering Light

Coming Up for Air

Grown from Sand

For Angela

Foreknowledge bleeds
twice behind the curtain,

knowledge shared
sheds pearls

—Paul Celan

An Unchartable Truth

A Crest of Memories

When the wind becomes
my heart and I undo
your eyes on night's
other edge, a bitter
taste floods my tongue
like a nub of tamarind.

The absence drinks
you dry and you re-
call the reasons
for forgetting and why, why
you've learned to sleep
in that shadow memory.

What is the sound of love
in this dark hour of death?
the look in your eyes
as you drift aside,
then far away in some
other knowledge where songs
suffused with lilacs and
blazing stars help you
die of such things?

Or, those absent figures
orbiting waters, most
tranquil the endless
returning in the shadow
of days where no out-
side nor inside pervades—

comforting like
wind through the pines,
then that glowing sadness
in the wrinkle of water as
we slip from the dream.

Coming up to eye-level,
we open the windows
and doors—and, finally,
let the d u s k enter.

Movements swallowed by the blue-green.

And Once Where Wind Was Born

Ancestral rhythms,
desolate voices.

That endless floating downstream
never again remembered,

but in those little songs
that pass like leaves,

songs like voices in the park,
rainbow variations.

The colors of a forest
once read in your palms—

Paper. Months.
Whispers, vespers.

A louvering light.

Cure me not to know.
Your fading face tightening,

thinning into mist,
growing ancient.

Feel the thirst, child.
That fading endlessly

into a mirror
of ourselves.

Could I Be Saying This in All My Own Voices?

Cold hand against blue skies

        Grey reason ticking

P r e m o n i t i o n s

hidden behind language

        speaking in tongues

Night, wise night

        my brush with death

that brush of death
in the mask of childhood

Keeper of shadows—

        shapemaker out of

nothing-
ness

        re-

        shaping

Somewhere time has returned to its noisy cities.

Sea Mist

Names drawn and objects
out of nothing, the shadow-

light in our bones,
the promise of music

through the hour-
glass, the light within the light.

Space, shapes, that falling heart
smothered in silence.

A bird coasting alone on the wind
waiting for language to arrive.

The ruins of the night,
torn, tattered, veiled, unveiled.

Distant Märchen.

Voices on the far side, blue
glances, splintered evergreens.

Deception. Future's heroism in love
with words, small hours,

ferocious void, instinct,
desire, animal rhythm.

Embrace it and the other spaces,
full of noise that utterance

of flight turning into water.

We are fearlessly swallowed by spray and mist and then renewed in some bygone fable called "The Marlin and The Whale."

Nephesh

I. Human Order

Dim prophecies.
Infernal blush;
and then finally, reprieve.

The true indifference
of those colors. Conscious-
ness preparing for death.

Strange alliance
rejects
that state of terror.

Words within hands
barely written. Words
demanding more.

Grim details. Everything in
the interim. Staring head on
into the eyes of a sun.

II. Congregations

Amassing a mass *en masse*,
and when night emerges,
from death, death.

Is it a tragedy to be
inhabited by parasites?
Surely everything is interior.

An ancient fear, primordial
almost. Therefore all this
flesh and bone armoring the heart?

The forest, the ocean,
the mountain—also
all daunting, no?

And who has the most ferocious eyes?

a reclining figure sighs;
and suddenly as if by magic,

at that unsure moment,
everything transforms
and we burst into song.

There's no sense in being tethered,
as the water falls and scatters like ashes.

Here no eddy or pool is clear.
The mirror reflects not the depths but the darkness.

Stories Seen in the Carvings

I. Whose Eyes Are Closed?

Slow beginnings
early mornings.

As clouds disperse,
the sky unravels;

ahead, voices
wrap around trees,

nudging streams
and whispers.

*What is the color
of water now?*

A great solidarity
dwells in light—

and in spare branches,
eternity finds a sound.

The clacking
of nail on wood,

and in the fog,
it's snowing leaves.

The breeze, a sniffle.
A cloth of light descends.

II. *The Concealed Motors of Narrative*

Aron't we made of light
both ahead and behind?

Dawnbreak,
the furnace burns.

The frames served on a door.
Fevered speech.

I would die if I were a rodent.

What a climate
to come home to.

What should move
ahead or through?

Heed the words
and dream them, Creature.

Wavering daybreak
from where black reigned alone.

Knotted brows sipping old wine,
tangled in the future-thought-of.

       (As if something we call flint
        might ink this all into infinity.)

And a train passes, sounding
like a predatory creature
seeking out a distant life.

Together we are
encased, enclosed
in a photograph,

a reel that unwinds
on pillowcases,
blithely saying

Touch me,
and the frond

of a leaf or petal,
innocently living inside, says,

Let me stroke you too.
That rising-up

through storm and weave,
clearly executed, seems

to explore
in a single together.

So then, why look back, my love?

Behind this canvas there is another sea of still and clear blue.

III. Intensive Care Unit

Vaguely abysmal, the city,
though our earthly architect
did his very best,

something's amiss—
the rattle of the furnace,
the hum of the vent

sends that hollow howl
through the inside of
the room

where another kind of snow,
a night snow, follows
childhood paths—

as in the purest form,
the ruse of a wandering life.

Slant veil of light mist
across hilltops now.

Words dressed with lemon
and mint float inside the mind
and the partnership wanders

through caverns
of absentee bats.
The silken sky plunges

toward the shore
where swollen seabirds
dart and dangle,

and the wave's white eye
stares on—a seamless pattern
dapples the sands,

sifting through
light to retrace
our fading tracks.

Wind never shapes the same way twice.

First Astronaut on Jupiter

The glisten, listen,
globular collusion,
that crackle. In a w e

at the waves of peroxide
frothing, snorting
across the s h o r e.

A ring of stones
immersed in a spiral
of silence on fields of i c e.

      To be the very first stone.

And the sunlight faintly
steals like a f o x
behind another ring of stones.

Your heart is torn
as a fleeting moment
of fire burns the atmosphere

from this Milky Way of young souls.
But where, you ask, is the driftwood
picking up on the shore?

and the surge of the sluggish
river winds down,
slowing vapors, shadows ... Listen,

you can hear the years
sifting through the bedrock,
falling into the bottom

of ourselves
while the earth
thrusts quietly ahead,

and the murmur
of her forest at night
and the h o l l o w walls of air,

the calls of the drunken dove,
the ticking of ants
moving their cities
halfway across the world.

And, still as dragon clouds,
these dawn waters, this land
of untouched s n o w s.

The aura that never dissolves. The rudder that leaves no wake.

Dance of Spring Water

Our starting point—
within the haze
of pinched fingers,
within the wild daffodils
as the pear trees lumber
in their centuries.

Our slow crawl
across an ocean
of wild grass
and the spiders collecting
dew in their webs
and in their fangs.

Washed ashore,
that sturdy pear,
yellowed, bruised
and battered, falling
through earth
and deep into

the breath of our words.
Sudden crosswind
as the rack
of a roebuck
peers over the horizon—
a darting here and there—

sparrows vie
for the last perch,
for the best perch.
Lights burn
through the curtain,
and the creature is away.

Artificial Flowers

Silk sense
woven

into ribbons.

The bees
are confused.

Then, the poetry
downstairs

as sunlight
breaks

through the scaffolding
where smeltings
drift from the city ...

as the horizon shifts
out toward

further

constellations.

The forms life takes as it vanishes and reappears, then as it dissolves.

Disillusion

Blue overflowing from the forests.

The froth of the creek.

Under the cover of trees,
a man sleeps—dreaming
of a room within a house

on a hill—so deep
he will never remember
the days and nights before.

There on the washed wall
of the forgotten,
composed of letters
describing the absolute,

that thinking of the thought
with conflict
before the thought awakens.

Two parallels fleetingly meeting.

In this state of being alone,
every sentence
repeats the past.

♦

Geese migrate blindly
into the cataract of a sun.

Oil Sheen

Driving into desert country
along the straight-tracked
manmade road.

Ahead, a canyon billows
dust-smoke, words
tremble in the lobe,

an old melody
whirs deep in the bone.
Light rises—or an illusion of it.

Ahead, a field
of weed wavers
lingers.

Rusting water silos
with perched crows.
Serpents snaking

somewhere below.
and the carcass of a hillside
emotionlessly reflects

the mountains. Yes,
shade, but where
the underlying matter?

and where is that fresh water
we saved for this evening?

Is there a magical phrase that can open water?

Clams

See the island in your mind
or you will always be lost.

Somehow we turn to stone in the presence of the breathing sea.

Meteor Showers

and as the dream reaches
out toward us

darkness falls again.

A wheel spins
in the unknown engine.

At the end
of the hall
a figure of
a man arrested

in a murmur
of voices.

That man is
carved stone

facing
ocean.

The seagulls tear toward thundering waters and drink in all the voices.

Summer's Surface

Crackling in
its gnarled edges
and warmed kinks,

we slip through
the noose of home
and prance out

into the white sails
of the big outdoors
where insects

are performing
in their whole-
some blue.

Water rises to touch the light, the eyebeams of the sun.

Cosmic Impulse

She tells me

> how ocean
> is the memory

of all things

> thought, think-
> ing, con-

sidered—how

> the sea seethes
> in its impulse

to capture each

> fleeting
> instinct

to transmute

> thought into
> side-

real time ...

To Discover Descartes

To discover the discarded,
the forgotten, or once

purveyed—in part, toxic,
the heart of a word

slithering toward small truths
under a starry sky.

And those thousand eyes
of mammalian

longing. O, to sleep
among the scavengers and predators,

but alive in the dark,
obliterated in the pavilions

of the insects, in the wake
of pollen and fragrance,

everything filled in and used,
but barely used up. The sparkles

that catch the light of the passing
cars or trucks carting

consciousness, or perhaps,
more aptly, a self-

consciousness edging toward
the warmth of morning.

Fantastic to feel
how the earth growsback into itself,
pushing itself back

toward the past, toward
the occan like a memory

transmuted or a deep
loneliness caving in

on itself, where every
thing is water, where

everything

sinks.

The brine, the gusts, a game of sea creatures.

When life is a dry slope, the sea is our rancor.

Oysterfolk

The traffic doesn't slow;
the bling navigates

like porpoises' eyes
in the windows,

those deep dangling metaphors
in a city tangled up in its own

industrial age, its charging up,
its injecting spaces

into the straits,
into the lost shipwrecks

where doubloons pay
deeper oceangoing figures.

To dissolve into the circle, wandering the pledge of faith,
sensing the backwash, nothing else.

Ringing in the New Year

In abandoned shacks
that once served

oysters to anglers
and fish to oysterfolk

high in the oven
of lunchtime.

Now, the sun
elbows in through tilted slats

and the hollow
wind calls out for

auld lang syne, my Jo.
For auld lang syne.

Foam-crested furrows, a hollow howl that shears the sails,
the gales of spirits swarming from sea to earth.

Warm Waters

Went to sleep for hours
until I heard the footsteps

in the hall downstairs.
The cat scratched the door

for fifteen seconds,
then the battle in the mind.

Outside in the garden
someone else slept.

It rained in my hands
and a huge tree

laden with moths
filled my head.

Stubborn creature—
you whistled over my bed.

and me, with my stuck-together eyes,
I rose from the dead,

and you pulled me gently
into the light, and

with loose fingers,
stirred whirlpools.

Days as years in this voracious luxuriant sea.
The rainfall a gauze curtain ending a line of sight.

A Crossing

The bridge observing
the greenery, water

coursing in-out—
waiting for the fish, or

minuscule signs of
life, flickering over

the surface, observing
the hurl—twigs

nosing stones
to the outskirts

of the riverbanks,
a transitional place

where flocks of geese
congregate in reeds—

pushing through mist,
looking down into

the silt, across the
flats where seeds

struggle to find foothold,
where swifts ignite—

the humming of the stones,
the sky an open mouth

yawning at the world
its dialects of blue

and green,
at the divided

wilderness
lost

in the
trees.

The coast a knife, the birds driving higher and beyond.

Here the Fragment of a Kiss

Caught
on camera
years ago.

Right there
under your
birthmark,

beneath your
cheekbone
in that space

you called *rigidity*
and the warmth
that rose

from the pit
of your gut
in a wave of red,

that blush
of contentment
an impossible rhetoric,

the splinter
of a life
well known.

To rise
from the underworld
and reach the frontier

all a-glare
in the faces of friends
and foes reading

in between
the lines, the hypnosis
of hydroponics

and the lined-up
ancient monkey heads,
the goats, nose against

panes, the ridged horns
clanking on glass and
the windows bursting wide.

Darkness hanging
deep-down,
are all moving parts

transparent,
asleep
at the wheel.

◆

We are sycamore trees,
all fingers
stretching into a sky.

We are paths, traveled,
warmed perhaps
on horseback;

perhaps we walk
the solemn and absurd
on all fours—

and all the tracks, the trails
we drag

through the melting
snow, through this

oh-so-hallowed
ground.

Billows, bellicose rippling—the dark mirror,
a streak, pulls away, pulses green.

The Dark Mirror

Silence w
        o
         r
           m
             s
its way down
into the streets.

Only at this time
can things be de-

cided

when no one can tell
ghost from shadow.

Rectangles in gloomy colors,
invisible the w o r d s

on fluttering banners,
or the broken arm
of faith

        f a i t h l e s s l y

apportioning
       glitter and gold
in all measure.

Blame the sun
or the blossom

Flocked by foam and wave
where the mouth meets a
stream of prayers, the memory
of brick houses and the music
of restless souls

in your hand
or all the friends

who have gathered closer

      i n c a h o o t s.

Gravity's End

Before the forest
there was an ocean

and before the ocean
a stone,

but before the stone
there was only space

filling up with
ooze and light.

Heavenly, the universes
inside the mind;

devilish, each
single world.

*Here on the islands, no bold proposals, no hissing frenzy of afternoons
and evenings in the metropolis.*

City Lights

Dare I say, the labyrinth was in her—
the path memorized like choral verses
from childhood.

She glanced down toward the assembled,
hoping she too might impart
what she knew. A lifetime

taught her a little less than half,
reflected in her laughter,
strained at best. She imagined

him as a lighthouse in a maelstrom
of cross-currents, of unpredictable shallows—
pure tomfoolery,

of course, thinking of her own symbolic
discoveries as, too, the illuminations—
a faint roar deep

in her inner ear told her
                something wants to be known.
To her, though, words meant little anymore.

              Electric, the channels of runoff
              twisting through the once-primordial forest,
              and the smoke emerges from funnels

              spilling out words on the sky: *Please don't die.*
              Calm consideration requires just the margins
              of a newspaper—something dragged under

the noses of authorities in their paralyzing
pinstripes.
                              Who lectures on death anyway?
It's all about the dying or those stasis chambers

frozen cryogenic in the chorus
of the patriarch, the wind that bellows
in its incontinent rain or sister snail

in her slow skate across the melting ice
of uneven waters.
                              Present is this island,
                              the cracking face of a perpetual cold.

We remember her still, even through
all the dark clouds in her chipped tiles
when people were carried by a wave

through their generous ghettos
and found their fates along the barriers
of truth. Could we walk along

the alleys singing, waving our masks
among the machines of virtue and vice,
spreading our salt fondly and

intrepid through curved space.
Eventually, the cold will hit her eyes, and
just for a second, she will see

her other face boldly clearing
the way down to   the waterfront.

Limbo Returns

*The hunt is the metaphor
into the heart of life.*

Dreaming the Beautiful

and once again thoughtful
winter rumbles toward us

as we walk home

under the signs that praise
the stark skyline,

the garbage cans littering

driveways, the swarms
of passing cars—

weightless we descend

the incline into the future,
the souls beneath the grass

giving little thought

to our ongoing intrusions.
How ripe the air smells,

condensed in silent promises.

Is there something else
we can trust, something

other than the air?

To stand still in the
twilight, the moisture

sticking to our palms,

to feel the city becoming
its heavy breathing

and those figures
slipping

deep into the dark
allure of Friday night.

Rainswept in a stormcloud, a stream of violins
as the lightning cuts the abyss

To Exist as Mirage in the Vapor of Her Dream

The fluttering of wings
in this part of the forest

where there's no turning
around—or on the beach,

in that crowd
of the unremembered,

an old freighter,
once a healthy giant,

now rocks forgotten
by all but these ravens.

Does everything dissolve into a mist of vapor and wind?

A Deathly Quiet

pervades the memory,
a pause—or pauses
in succession, as if

a frigid chill vibrates
deep in the bones,
as if a Master of Lies

claps his hands—or
rubs them against each other,
as brother clasping brother—

a knowing hinted at,
a reaping of dead skin cells;
and then, the illimitable silence

that once was, breaks—
flies apart, as if
the memory may only be

an imagined past
or the word abused
in context is nothing.

*In a brief fluttering of curtains, the limbo returns
as his failed prodigy traverses oceans.*

Drawing on Lives Past

In these luminous spaces
where valley meets sea,
you wait for a friend
and the morning's pale light
swathes the mountain
with thoughtful language.

It's too early still,
what's visible, not awake,
what's awake, not yet visible.
What's audible is running
away with itself—
upwards, the stars still present,

winking into silence,
beginning their dream
of bone and flesh,
of dazzling storms,
an endless text
leaping from planet

to planet, flowers-
and trees- and fossils-
to-be, a power of such
beauty above and below in the pitch
beyond death, where worlds
are repainted again and over
in shadows, where a curious
child is hypnotized
by a future unknown—
and then, the dream
subsides and walks
into itself

four million times,
and sky flows into the room
on the edge of this space,
dreaming out of sight
or in the light for other eyes
high on the crest;

and judges nothing and gives
everything to oxygen.

Silent Prayer

How could I expect you
to climb out of your grave

and creep through
our old haunts

to stand beside me
and point out who walks

like a martyr,
who soars like a buzzard?

Your millions set adrift
in convoys headed

to the edge of death,
the moon above

and below, quantum
illusions, figurative

or literal expressions
of what is to come

and who is to haunt us—
winding down the track—

a countryside path
taken by all your

count-
less, your

count-
less old souls.

How bitter the taste of this breeze.

Forewarning

From the myth
which has no end
but is always transforming.

From the theft of fire
to the pursuit of a loved one
in the city of the dead, from

salvation from the flood
or the deep search for eternal
life where we are surrounded

by ourselves rather than the world—
from the missing patterns
of thought behind words.

*The prayers of many, the cold lights that seared the froth and the wave
that circled its islands, that lit the arm-length of humanity.*

Beneath the Heat

This earthly paradise
instinctively hides
in the shadows and sleeps.

> Does the dream
> that consumes forests
> and grassland, lays

> waste to insects and birds
> or leaps across fishless oceans
> only to build

> towering cities of glass
> and steel keep everything
> frozen in a single thought?

From this unlighted cabin window, the air unhooks itself and darts away.

Or the eddies—carrying households of plastics—
visible even here far from the machinations—
and, far from the labor strikes,
the bodies washed up after a storm.

Then, the Sand

Between everything:

Ground seashell stirring
in the color of twilight,

gestures of evolutionary thought
roaming, still unsettled

in waves of wind,

draughts of the fallen
arising once again to pester

and peek, to cry against
themselves, turning, turning

into erosion, eating away

the light, eating away

the bright

glass

Suffering Light

Everything runs backward here.
Forgive the time that beats against your wrist.

Suffering Light

Waves in the fields,
flaring feathers—

truth/non-truth,
cloud formations.

The girl in the picture:
a heavenly love—

and no one
sees the memory.

Half-here/half-not
in any book.

The theater of fear.

In a model incarnation,
white moonlight burns

behind the sun and the
alabaster serpent

stirring into action
swerves through the pasture

heaven-ready, drowning
in the knee-high grass.

Filled Out with Moonlight

A grazing of dust in this
tranquil, quilted time.

Eyes unseen, unknown.

Seaslugs and curled shells
moving in slow-postured mastery.

Veritably uniform, formed
in union, coming into darkness,

a heavier substance: the sub-
strate of the skies, of planets,

suns, space beyond space,
the concept of conception.

In the Amphitheatre

Where no rest delights
the wave of applause,

nutshells rattling, quilled,
half-awake, polyglots

cheer, their pangs
and potencies

assumed—what a beautiful
harness that rides the curtain-

call. So much for that,
that span of force

where the self-possessed
yowl across the balustrades,

flame-flickering, the
quivering of voices,

of words unwritten.
Evasion eviscerates.

Indulgence and insolence
escape like plasma.

Outside, harmonious cats
tread the pathway.

Each meeting facile,
each voice

intact and interred,
a delicacy stirring between

new and old,
sunrise and disdain,

broken, shattered, discarded
as the Risen rise again

far from the soil, its intelligence:
research shows

the Eastern voyage begins
where the ocean ends.

Where is that hand of evening when ocean touches the sky?

Extradimensional

The thought
grew back,
still more
bellicose,
full of caprice,
a smudged
design of
excursions
into experience.
Hapless words
that belie
the serene
and the sly, that ex-
hume a blue sky
turning purple,
and those
who pass
beneath,
believing sun-
shine grows
the bones,
anointing
their dreams
with jazz
quartets, pro-
nouncing pro-
nouns in
waltz time.

The strophes nourish beyond the rippling of straits—

Money Flaunts the Good Star

Boldly, in that rumbling
bottomness, a tender filigree
attune to the unison

of mothers and daughters,
a sound of bubbling felicity
as the grand curtain rises.

A second, similar counterpart
that's been carried over,
four voices out of the storm

naming a few things
for themselves, those buzzards
circling the carrion, the

broad-handed undertaker
clucking, clicking his tongue.

Look at the lavender curls!
The bodies quivering like
mercurial fluid, moving toward

those overgrown hands
and the flickering of the candle
on the nightstand: everything

made visible, again.

And into the deep sleep of finned creatures.

Counting Cards

In their manner of address,
grace accompanied

by a radiant moon, long
before daybreak, shortly

before the clouds
begin their vespers,

the ghosts of old comedy
forget their former lives,

in their surrendered wake
they forget to set the traps

for those drifting into sleep—
instead they ply their solitaires

and their spangled
and their garbled opinions.

That lunar flock over an ocean calm.

Price of Sunday Morning

Even in the clouds,
along the telephone poles,

on the tin roofs of desolate beach shacks,
in the trash cans, the birds;

paradise an unwound clock—

a timeline without curve.

Swallows, dear creature,
are breaking up in hues.

An hourglass measuring not with sand, but the unnerving liquid which
fills every exposure, every filament, every crack.

In Place of Success

Perpetual motion
in mid-sentence,

incarceration of
witnesses, the bold

verily viewing
the largesse in the house

of the metaphysician, in the bone
marrow of late evening,

the unrepentant in green,
the mirror of day reflecting

dead summer,
stillness sprinkled

in the heat of the asphalt;
in the land of the long-gone,

a place of great bounty,

the side of the road:
silt collects the sun's comforts,

a slow chain
of amino acids

whispers
in the puddle.

That receding arc of land, the roof, the dome alone in the dark.

Starred in the Margins

Mother of gods,
imagine yourself

as an explanation,
raised on the wall,
a carved star

shimmering through glass
in a blazing trail

of epiphanies—
a dominion as tall

as a cloud, like nothing
else, a breath-full

of beautiful thoughts
of sorrow and dread.

A Whole World Acclimated

Somehow the antithesis
of Insect, stirred into half-figures
where treasures
appreciate an academic death,
where a purple slip
in autumn, lewder
than this sky,
is a part of all things,
and a sky that does not bend
or turn, even when the frost,
naked in the sun,
deceives the moon.
And that helpless laughter,
so full of summer,
magnolias, and the songs
of rugged lands closely
bedding, even wedding each other
and the kisses breast
distances as far as sleep,
as far as i d e a s.

Follow the squall, a gentle trail, deep into the pitch.

Summer, So Full

Not the noble storm
of sunlight,
            but the last doe-eyed
days, the thing in itself,

            falcons coasting
on updrafts,
            bougainvillea in bloom
and the dark high-res
            glimmering indigo.

In this flash of indecision
            the lips reach
for the warmed body
            and the neck turns
toward shadow.

            The rattling in the leaves
as your dress
            settles in your lap—
and heavenly, precious
            light breathes between
the louvered trees,
            all eyes gaze upward
addressing the clouds
            and their cloudwork,
a music without sound
            drifts us into waking dreams—
a magnetism
            stirring the head
and in the feet,
            sorrow, fiction

        just days before the fall,
before the swollen garden
            flickers out,
before the moon rises

clear out of your skull.

The Secret Affinities of Pollen

Angry ideologies,
flimsy stuff,

but when vanity
drops its guard

the secret affinities
are pollen,

hymns, unbelief touching
a hidden nerve.

The glint
of marketed images,

ideas of freedom,
democracy,

the big myth of history
where one

plunges into pre-
consciousness,

deeper:
betrayal and breakdown,

longing and defeat,
the vein

of knowing or
not-knowing.

A homespun pride
raises the rust,

a bravado
where no one

gets what was so
idly stated—

the blinders
that hold one

from fear,
the assimilations

of hodgepodge,
the yielding,

the withheld,
the water-

rounded edges
of the mind

where flux
is the master,

conventions
rearranged

in order
of appearance.

Time weighs inward
in encounters

with the divine,
the ever-looking-

over-the-shoulder
for that space

between—
for the paradoxes,

for that shadow
within light.

Coming Up for Air

*Can time be regained
in a sea of sleep?*

Warpaint

A murderous sunrise.

All-night-fighting
with the dead.

A speech resumes—
no, a stern lecture
of a kingdom

once had, the
homicidal falling
at the feet and the eyes

all alleys, all
in your twenties.
Hackneyed, perhaps—

perhaps
hand-on-heart
fleeting.

Sunlight looking for forms to fill the day.

*Is it just some trick of light that leaves become birds
and fly off into an absent ocean?*

(A Feather Fallen from its Ocean-Bound Wing
Swirls Onward, Onward ...)

(The so-called verve
of a childish churlish tirade—
the Pacific Ocean tide

coming into the shores of your mind.
Oh, to be a hermit crab
on a dune above the sea,

the dichotomy of privacy
and the money spent
on the sanctity of visions.)

Expecting the wind might extinguish you.

A Photograph

Thread
       b a r e art

         to lie

           in wait

     for t h e l i g h t

             to p e e l away

        its dark

       m
       y
       s
       t
       e
       r
       i
       e
       s

But having the sea to yourself and wanting to stride across the water.

Mysteries

Suspended in a blue-white sky,
threatened from beneath

by those fist-wielding locals,
(a bird as the word of a god)—

and just as they had been washing
their feet, the seepage of

the stagnant water
and the burning black cloud of oil—

Curtains! they roar
in that guttural, centuries-old tongue,

clinging to the edges,
like summer snows on

mountain chains—transcendent
in their wetlands, their harsh marshes.

What is this foolish stunt
where quicksand breathes

those shallow breaths
that snuff out toads?

What is reflected in the eye?
That careless slipping,

the light turning the tree.
the dazzle, the dapple,

a shaking that keeps you
steady like grass, and

the night—when creatures
reemerge to catch sleeping flies.

Again, the sky plucks at bursts of cloud.

Far Planet

A sky tilted toward the world
blooming in phosphorescence,

but where to begin
once moving.

To shuffle toward
those odd angles

where the membranes
of space bend and curve

and the snow
that once was,

is imagined
in a room

with the ashes
and the silence by the fire.

How young
we seem

in that old weight
of inexorable hours.

Now the Moon Sinks Too

Behind the light
there is a strong
smell of evening.

Faces appear
against the dark
like masks.

Somehow we
still feel
the sea's will.

Love should be born
out of this gloss
of blackness,

and yet we want to
climb out
to see a sky

the color of water
and trees, trees
everywhere.

Grown from Sand

Forlorn until Noon

Briefly sad, the grasses
drooping, staring

at their roots, bowed
under the current;

as if in wishing to say
what they would have liked to,

the tears have gathered at
the tips of their questioning heads.

This is Forever: the tuna chasing minnows.

Karma

How the birds have stopped singing,
how the green has become gray,

how your last words resonate
—this is the very thing you are.

A short note from the heart.
I could still hear his laughs

from where while reading
at the kitchen lamp, the night

was windowless and the words
split apart as the housefly drilled

into the cracks, but there was grace
here in its silent voluptuousness

bearing down upon my breast
like an ocean, ignorant, old and

preserving; and hunched I walked
the narrow passage into the dreams

of my dreams, afraid of what it meant
to be orphaned, to be departed,

or the money spent on acquiring identity
and the light that louvers

in the *I do*, in the shuffling of thought
between the latter and the former,

and the fate of family or the smell
of consequence in all its sizes—

flooded in impartial stares:
how the nearsighted cloud in the pane

has little fear of the unknown,
and the illusion of will in the small

gentle order recalls the belligerent,
the delinquent, the crushed

genes of atomic time,
where such small quarry

was the pastime of lesser
gods, of forest spirits

or water fry, where the sky
forks away and we were

reborn again, every second
Sunday among the birds.

Perhaps I am the only ghost to haunt this place.

The Meaning Of

In love with statues,
pictures of faces
moving into the moonlight,

that strange reaction
echoing, stirring
the seeds of a glossy memory

where the strong scents
of sweat and strife
squat in the dark

and childish happiness
lingers like a torn piece of cloth
on a hook or a nail—

a nail that once held
an image of your own face,
stoic, steady, sullen.

The mind slips into its cells
where the future is part
of the old view ...

What if, from the hospice window
along the causeway,
when out into a calm

unstirring sea,
matter swaps with
matter, and delicious strands

of kelp bloom and rise
with their eyes
wide open?

And your silence will conform to you.

Wheels of Industry

Light turns blue, turns old.

The gears and cogs roar.

Nailed to clouds,
the dying float above.

Drained, we emerge
from stained glass

among the trees
raising arms, singing.

As the dust rises,
the sky falls, and the grain

nestles in our pockets.

Still waiting to catch the next best gust of wind.

Enchantment on the Islands

It was cold, and
the mud under my feet

was peeling
away at my heels

like a black sap
oozing toxins.

My eyes caught
a movement in the trees ...

A quivering, some-
thing slipping in and out

of consciousness, then
the iron whiff of blood

in a soft-rolling
of wind tides,

when someone suddenly
took my hand

and drew me through
the wave of weeds.

As far as the tarnished
tinsel she led me,

through a thin tangle of myself
she led me, no maps

no sense or hint
of technology,

and we tumbled
in the grasses and the leaves

mirroring the quilts
of clouds, to a space

where joy and awe communed,
and soon, we sprouted

wings, clamoring
for distance, for that burning

in our eyes, the winds
pressing down upon us

from every side
as we soared toward

an open ocean, and passing
horses holding to

the courage of the land,
we drowned

and we burned out,
whirling into

our other
selves.

Or perhaps things are discovered only when you breathe on them?

Species of Light

Intuition shaping as
a physical act, then
(moving into the future of itself)

and shuffling into
the space before language
(the muscular structure of emotion)

that is reflected, refracted—
(being seen by the future
in the reflection).

The not-yet-yet-not
letting go/setting free
(of profitability).

(Deep time in millions of years)
capitalizing on those
momentary capillaries of light.

Ecosystem of an Anonymous Machine

For the machinery of the world
is much too complex
for the simplicity of men. —Borges

What is the interface
of the natural world?

Mind caught in the act.

Regret turned into disgrace.

The pity of deceit when light
breaks in indifference.

Or the magnitude of a mind
bending at will. To what though?

The stuff of theater?

Confusion when the breath
snuffs out.

What is wickedly divine?

and then, awakened again
by some fear that the old way,

the nameless paths cross restlessly
where gods recite short poems

behind this space, suspended
and boundless, the doors shut.

Then, the ball begins, and we
dance, we dance in earnest.

Are my eyes the same blue
they once were?

The loose cobbles are shifting:
some secret everywhere.

I pause, take in the air—
sensing what it once was,

pause again at the roots
of a building planted

with firm reason; the sky blurs,
the source of the thing

drained away in the ruts and gutters
of the city. *Heaven be assuaged.*

The hectic has gone.
The urban longing,

the pitiful trees along
the boardwalk, the full beginning,

the dirt under nails, the kissing
strangers, the drinkers

and their fine wine imported
from distant shores. Still,

the stone glistens, even
as my lips grow numb.

Is it just that I yearn for a gentle immersion?

A Brew

Concocted where love was
      just yesterday.

Vague to me, yet
      an image made
in a hotel room.

      That form of days
turned into years.

The end, so it began.

Don't say anything at all.

Simply watch the outline
      of the trees

and the clouds restlessly
      clutching the cold night.

Is being at the heart of knowing or knowing at the heart of being?

Even after everything else, still a figment in the light.

Every Subterfuge

Almost mute, rumpled,
ruffled, exhilarated
in the river's whistle,

everything seems full.
A mildness, a calm ...
then you materialize,

sighing as if in love.
The ocean streams off
your back, a layer of wild.

How much has sunk in,
bled into your pores
over the years: the salt,

the hard calcified shells,
the ink of invertebrates—
it fills you with clear, warm

blue, and all the waters
in tight embrace,
the voices borderless,

the tones tied in knots
then freed again, pieces
of a puzzle spread through

another heaven where almost
everything flies, fragments,
plumes and scars

drift in all directions.
A deep reverberation in
the clinking, the scuffling,

the scratching of shell
upon shell, body
etched upon body.

Surprised by the bounty
of voices in the upswell.

What about when the audience leaves and you're left with only yourself.

Ill-Gotten Ways

A Reflection

Fire turns the corner
among the reeds
down at the waterline.

Is there a word for this?
When solids burn alongside
liquids? and the shallows

so insincere, run to
snatch up the leftovers.
Where's the risk in that?

To take the half-devoured,
half-charred remains—
but then—a big nevertheless,

wind, flight, curve.
Air is everywhere
devouring every morsel,

stirring up the essences
to make them new.
The heart of a mirror.

Lauded for all their radiance—
flies swarm the magnitude.
Even the guiltiest of us

have someone to protect,
and thus, rose or lichen,
ostrich or oyster,

each of us wants to fly—
the cypress, the cinnamon tree,
the olive, the briefest

stalk of parsley wavering,
quivering in excitement
at the shriek of a kestrel,

the wail of a buzzard,
the thunderclap, deep
in our innermost ear.

Once I thought I had found the Metaphysical Substance.

Nacre

Popular and peopled like a sneeze,
the returning ones

are a cloud dreaming,
a joke retold.

Suffering the glow
of growing dull.

Don't you wonder why
through all this
giving way to elbows and tears—

corruption survives, hell
thrives—and models
everything on old deals.

Tomorrow they say
will be purer, more radiant.

Tomorrow we soar
on stolen wings.

Electrocuting Nights

An idiom is a thief,
a fine-mesh filter

for man's burden of grief.
The dead must be

laughing on their heads,
making wild displays
in their earthly hackles.

To outshine
the wrinkles of winter,

always summer,
bold and blooming,

these are the moon's
seeds. To mirror the joy
of ten thousand seas.

What would it take to break
into blossom, dear creature.

Drop into your forehead
and dwell awhile.

Grasp your partner's wrist,
stroll the streets as nobody else.

Turn and face each other.

To put flesh on the white-bone of light,
to encounter air as a cool liquid thought.

Notes:

"Warm Waters" is for Miriam.

"City Lights" is for Charlie Chaplin and Emily Dickinson.

"The Meaning Of" is for my mother, Angela Margaret Seach-Vincenz, born in Teddington, England, died in Williamstown, MA, USA, in 2017, now buried under Milly's apple tree in Cheshire, MA, overlooking Herman Melville's Greylock Mountain.

"Extradimensional" is after Wallace Stevens.

"Nacre" is after John Ashbery.

Many thanks to Dennis Maloney and Elaine LaMattina, and White Pine Press.

Acknowledgments:

Many thanks to the editors of the following publications where these poems previously appeared:

New American Writing 38:
"To Discover Descartes" and "A Deathly Quiet"

New American Writing 39:
"Suffering Light" and "Karma"

Colorado Review:
"Stories Seen in the Carvings"

Another Chicago Magazine:
"Dreaming the Beautiful," "Beneath the Heat," and
"In the Amphitheatre

Evergreen Review:
"The Secret Affinities of Pollen," "Warpaint," "Starred in the Margins,"
and "Money Flaunts the Good Star"

Solstice:
"Oil Sheen"

Art and Letters:
"In Place of Success" and "Drawing on Lives Past"

Plume:
"Gravity's End," previously entitled "When Will the Last Apple Fall"

spoKe 6:
"Nacre," previously entitled "Gold," "A Brew," "Forewarning," "Silent
Prayer," and "City Lights"

spoKe 7:
"A Crest of Memories," "Nephesh," "Artificial Flowers," "Mysteries," "The Meaning Of, "and "Every Subterfuge"

Unlikely Stories Part 5:
"Extradimensional," previously entitled "Commencement"

Beltway Review:
"Far Planet"

Axon: Creative Explorations (Australia):
"First Astronaut on Jupiter"

SurVision (Ireland):
"Ecosystem of an Anonymous Machine"

Fortnightly Review (France):
"Species of Light," "Wheels of Industry," "Forlorn Until Noon," "Now the Moon Sinks Too," and "Counting Cards"

On the Seawall:
"Summer, So Full"

Tourniquet Review:
"Price of Sunday Morning"

I-70 Review:
"Ill-Gotten Ways"

Several poems from this collection were first performed on *Lit Balm,* the livestream reading series (www.litbalm.org).

The Author

Marc Vincenz is a poet, fiction writer, translator, editor, musician and artist. He has published over 30 books of poetry, fiction and translation. His more recent collections, include, *A Brief Conversation with Consciousness, The Little Book of Earthly Delights, There Might Be a Moon or a Dog,* and *39 Wonders and Other Management Issues.* His work has been published in *The Nation, Ploughshares, Raritan, Colorado Review, Washington Square Review, Fourteen Hills, Willow Springs, Solstice, World Literature Today, The Los Angeles Review of Books* and many other journals. He is publisher and editor of MadHat Press and publisher of *New American Writing,* and lives on a farm in Western Massachusetts where there are more spiny-nosed voles, tufted grey-buckle hares and *amoeba scintilla* than humans.

OTHER WORKS BY MARC VINCENZ

POETRY

The Propaganda Factory, or Speaking of Trees
Mao's Mole
God's of a Ransacked Century
Behind the Wall at the Sugarworks
Beautiful Rush
Additional Breathing Exercises (Bilingual:German-English)
This Wasted Land and Its Chymical Illuminations (annotated by Tom Bradley)
Becoming the Sound of Bees
Sibylline (illustrated by Dennis Paul Williams)
The Syndicate of Water & Light
Leaning Into the Infinite
Here Comes the Nightdust
Einstein Fledermaus
A Brief Conversation with Consciousness (illustrated by Sophia Santos)
The Little Book of Earthly Delights
There Might Be a Moon or a Dog
39 Wonders and Other Management Issues
The King of Prussia is Drunk on Stars
The Form of Time: New and Selected Poems
A Splash of Cave Paint

LIMITED EDITIONS AND CHAPBOOKS

Benny and the Scottish Blues (illustrated by D. Dewan)
Genetic Fires
Upholding Half the Sky
Pull of the Gravitons

TRANSLATIONS

Kissing Nests by Werner Lutz
Nightshift / An Area of Shadows by Erica Burkhart and Ernst Halter
A Late Recognition of the Signs by Erica Burkhart
Grass Grows Inward by Andrea Neeser
Out of the Dust by Klaus Merz
Secret Letter by Erica Burkhart
Lifelong Bird Migration by Jürg Amman
Unexpected Development by Klaus Merz
An Audible Blue: Selected Poems 1963-2016 by Klaus Merz
Casting a Spell in Spring: Selected Poems by Alexander Xaver Gwerder

FICTION

Three Taos of T'ao or How to Catch a Fortuitous Elephant
City of Lemons